POUR IT OUT

Letters to My Heavenly Father about Grief

ERICKA FINLEY

Copyright © 2025 Ericka Finley

All rights reserved. No part of this publication may be reproduced, distributed, or transmitted in any form or by any means, including photocopying, recording, or other electronic or mechanical methods, without the prior written permission of the publisher, except in the case of brief quotations embodied in critical reviews and certain other noncommercial uses permitted by copyright law.

ISBN: 979-8-9937435-0-9

Edited by: I A.M. Editing, Ink

Book Cover & Interior Design: Book Design Stars

Dedication

To my daughter, Robyn Marie:

You were the light who broke through my darkest days. Thank you for giving me hope when my world was in pieces and love when my heart could not mend itself.

In Loving Memory of Two Hearts

Alexander Williams
04/21/87 – 2/28/2015

Robbie Williams
11/04/1971 – 12/02/2015

In loving memory of my mother, Robbie Wiliams, and my brother, Alex Williams, who both left this world in the same year but will never leave my heart. Your absence has carved a space in me that words can't fill, yet it is in that space that your love still lives and breathes.

Mom, your strength, wisdom, and faith taught me how to stand. Alex, your laughter and loyalty reminded me that I never walked alone. This book is a tribute to the lessons that you all gave me, the dreams you encouraged, and the courage you helped me find when life felt unbearable. Every page carries a piece of you both, and as long as these words exist, your light continues forward. This is for you.

Forever In My Heart,

Ericka

Table of Contents

Foreword 6

Acknowledgements 8

Opening Blessing: May You Rest in His Healing 9

Introduction 10

Denial 12

Anger 25

Bargaining 38

Depression 50

Acceptance 64

Transformed by Grief 78

Letters of Legacy 81

Faith & Emotional Healing Tools 88

Scriptures for Grief & Comfort (ESV) 90

Pour It Out: Personal Grief Journal 92

Closing Prayer: Surrender and Renewal 118

Foreword

JUSTUS

My heart still hears the echoes of your love.
My body still feels the embrace of your hugs.
My life is still shaped by the memories that we made.
Nothing can separate me from your love, not even a grave
There is no eulogy for you and me
Because we are a beginning with no end—
My confidant, my mother, brother, friend
Sometimes life without you feels like an injustice, because it was just us for so long.
Then I remind myself that you are not gone.
You are in my shoulders when I stand tall.
You are in my tears when they fall.
You are in my daughter's smile.
You are in my son's handsome face.
Your presence is felt in the decisions I make,
My ability to handle adversity with grace.
I see you.
I look for you every day
Not a phone call away,
But in my DNA
The essence of everything that I am
And everything that I ever will be.
As I live, your love lives within me.

There are so many things that can be said about Ericka. Many would speak of her tenacity and resilience. Many would mention her brilliance or her empathy. Some might even say that she's a breath of fresh air. But I'd say she's oxygen; she breathed life into me when I thought my spirit was dying. She speaks hope into seemingly hopeless situations. That is truly her gift, a gift forged through overcoming her own life-shattering heartache. Piece by piece, God shaped her character during her grief. This book is a testament to that.

As you read, know that she earned every chapter written. I anticipate that this book will do for you what Ericka has done for me: it will show you how to breathe. I hope it breathes hope into your spirit. I hope that in your grief, this book allows you to feel the love of God and to trust that there is purpose in your pain. He is always doing something new, and even though you are brokenhearted, God still has plans for you.

Peace and Comfort,

Danielle Timmons

Acknowledgements

First and foremost, I give all glory to God, my Heavenly Father, for carrying me through the depths of grief and guiding every word of this book. His love and presence sustained me when my heart felt too heavy to bear.

To my husband, Brandon: thank you for your unwavering patience and love, and for holding space for me through every tear.

To my children: your laughter and joy reminded me daily of hope and God's promises, giving me the courage to keep writing.

To my dad, my bonus mom, Crystal, and my family—both biological and "work family": your prayers, love, and faith were steady anchors for my heart.

To my sister, Destiny: thank you for taking an idea and bringing it to life. This cover design is a tangible reflection of my journey. What an honor it has been to create this cover with you after walking through this grief journey side by side.

To my sister, Trina: thank you for capturing the echoes of my heart through your beautiful poem. God has truly gifted you with the ability to create beauty through words. It is both an honor and a blessing to have you write the foreword for this book.

To my therapist and my circle of friends: your encouragement, late-night prayers, and unwavering presence reminded me that I was never alone. You held space for my tears and celebrated every small step toward healing with me.

To my church family at Kingdom Purpose Ministries: thank you for creating a space where my gifts and anointing could flow freely. Your love and discipleship have nurtured my spiritual growth and shown what's possible when believers are united in purpose and rooted in God's love.

To the community I am birthing through The Strong Friend's Resting Place, LLC: this book reflects our shared mission—to encourage hearts, offer rest, and remind others that they are never alone in their grief.

Above all, may this work stand as a testament to God's faithfulness—proof that even in the valley, His love is enough, His promises are true, and His presence never leaves us.

May You Rest in His Healing

May peace find you in the quiet places.
May love remind you that you are never alone.
May every tear water something new—
A gentler strength, a deeper trust, a quieter hope.
When memories ache, may they also shine.
When the nights feel long, may his presence be your light.
And when you cannot see the way forward,
May his grace carry you until joy softly returns.
Your story is still being written.
Your heart is still capable of beauty.
And your God is still here—
Healing, holding, and making all things new.
"The steadfast love of the Lord never ceases;
His mercies never come to an end;
They are new every morning."
—Lamentations 3:22-23 ESV—

Introduction

When Grief Speaks and the Soul Laments

1 Peter 5:7: "Cast all your anxiety on him, because he cares for you."

Grief has a way of showing up uninvited, shaking everything you thought was certain. It is more than sadness. It is sorrow that settles in your chest, confusion that clouds your mind, and silence that stings in the presence of God. It is the ache of loss wrapped in layers of love, disbelief, anger, and longing.

For a long time, I thought grief had to be polished to be presented to God, that I had to come to Him healed or at least holding it together. But grief taught me otherwise. It taught me how to lament.

Lamenting is not just crying; it is crying out. It is the sacred act of bringing your honest, raw, and unfiltered emotions before the Lord. Lamenting is what David did in the Psalms, what Job did in his suffering, and what Jesus did in the garden of Gethsemane. It is the kind of prayer that does not always end in resolution but leads to a deeper relationship. It is when faith and pain sit in the same room and refuse to walk away from God.

Lamenting is not weakness. It is worship in the wilderness.

In these pages, I will walk you through the five stages of grief: denial, anger, bargaining, depression, and acceptance. But I will not just talk about them clinically. I will show you what they felt like for me. I will share the letters I wrote to God from each place of heartbreak and confusion. I did not always use pretty words. I did not always tie my letters up with faith-filled endings. But I was honest, and I believe God honors our honesty more than our performance.

Grief does not follow a straight line. These stages are not steps you check off; they are waves you survive. You may go back and forth between them. You may feel all of them in a single day. And that is okay.

My prayer is that, in reading my journey, you will find language for your own, that you will feel permission to be vulnerable with God, to cry out like the psalmist, to question, to wrestle, and still be held. Grief is not the absence of faith; it is often the proving ground of it.

So come with me, stage by stage, letter by letter. Let us grieve honestly. Let us lament boldly. And let us heal slowly, in the presence of a God who can handle every emotion we bring to Him.

Closing Prayer

Dear God,

I do not always have the words. Sometimes all I have is the ache in my chest and the questions that keep me up at night. But I bring them to You anyway. I bring the parts of me that are shattered, confused, angry, tired, and holding on by a thread.

Teach me how to lament. Teach me how to be honest with You without fear of rejection. Help me to see that I do not have to pretend in Your presence. You are not offended by my sorrow, You meet me in it. You do not require perfection, just my presence.

As I walk through the stages of grief, remind me that You are not only the God of joy but the God of tears. Help me find Your nearness in the middle of the mess. Give me grace to feel, space to mourn, and strength to hope again.

Even when I do not understand, help me trust that You are still good. Even when I am not okay, remind me that You are still with me.

In the name of the One who wept with us and for us, Jesus Christ, I pray.

Amen.

STAGE 1:
Denial

When reality feels too heavy to hold.

You whisper, "This can't be real," as your heart tries to protect itself from what your mind already knows. God is near, even in your disbelief—patient, gentle, and steady. He waits beside you, letting the truth settle one breath at a time.

I am *safe* to face what I once avoided. God meets me here.

Denial: When Reality Feels Impossible

Introduction

This letter comes from the stunned, disbelieving place of grief, where your mind refuses the new, terrible truth and you keep looking for the exit from the nightmare. Denial is not the absence of feeling; it is the heart's attempt to protect itself from being shredded all at once.

Letter to God

Dear God,

This cannot be my life.

There is no way that I have served You all my life only to face this kind of heartbreak. My brother was murdered. Never, never in a million years did I expect a phone call telling me he had been gunned down in the street.

I stood there, staring at his blood on the pavement, completely numb. I could not believe it then, and I still cannot believe it now. I cannot believe You allowed his life to end this way. I cannot believe You let them take him from us.

How am I supposed to help my mom survive this? How am I supposed to keep his legacy alive or help raise his two sons? I am only twenty-five, a broke college student just trying to survive myself. How am I supposed to carry all of this?

God, I do not understand. I know You had the power to save him. There are stories everywhere of people surviving after being shot multiple times. You saved them. Why did You not save my brother? That question haunts me. Why did You not intervene? Why would You think we are strong enough to handle this pain? Because I am not. I am not strong enough for this.

Sitting in that funeral home, helping pick out a casket for my brother, watching my mother weep uncontrollably, I have never felt so helpless. That image is forever etched into my memory. I will never be able to call him again. I will never hear his laugh or crack jokes with him until we cry from laughter. Instead, I am picking out clothes for him to wear for his memorial service.

Seeing him lying in that casket, so still, so peaceful, did not feel real. It felt like I was trapped in a nightmare, just waiting for someone to wake me up. Even now, I replay everything in my mind and ask myself, How did I get here? Why is this a chapter in my story?

I know You. I serve You. I believe in You. I go to church. I pray. I try to live right. I am supposed to be Your daughter. So why would You allow my family to experience this level of pain? I am trying, truly trying, to trust You and not lean on my own understanding, but I am struggling.

It is hard to trust when I feel like I have been forgotten. It is hard to trust when I know I did not deserve this. None of us did. God, please help me understand the why. I do not have peace. I do not have clarity. But I still want to believe You are with me, even in this. Please help me hold on.

Love,

Ericka

Takeaway

Denial does not mean you do not care; it means the pain is too fresh to accept all at once. It is okay to feel stunned, to ask "why," and to sit in the unknown. God does not punish our confusion; He meets us in it, tenderly holding the parts we cannot hold ourselves.

Scripture (ESV)

Psalm 34:18: "The Lord is near to the brokenhearted and saves the crushed in spirit."

Prayer

Lord, my heart is numb and the world feels unreal. I am struggling to make sense of this loss and to trust You in the middle of it. Come close to us now, wrap my mother and family in Your presence, steady our hearts, and give us the strength to keep going one moment at a time. Help me to hold on when I cannot feel hope. Amen.

Denial: When the World Feels Unreal

Introduction

This letter comes from the stunned, disbelieving place when the moment of truth does not match the prayers you have whispered. Denial is not a refusal to feel; it is a mind and heart trying to protect themselves from a reality that feels impossible to hold.

Letter to God

Dear God,

What is the point of praying if You were not going to honor my request? I specifically prayed that You would not take my mom away. I remember it like it was yesterday.

I was sitting in the courtroom, waiting for them to call my case. I was working for DCF at the time and had a shelter hearing. Suddenly, I felt a gut-wrenching pain in my stomach, panic overtook me, and I just knew something was wrong. I tried calling my mom several times, but she did not answer. I called my sister and asked if she had talked to Mom that day. She had not. So I called my grandmother, who was living with my mom, and asked her to go check on her. I just knew in my spirit that something was wrong.

As my grandmother agreed to go check, they called my case, and I had to hang up. I walked into the courtroom whispering a silent prayer, begging You to protect my mom. I told You I could not handle losing her.

When I came out of court, I had several missed calls from my aunt. When I finally got her on the phone, she told me I needed to come home because my grandmother had gotten sick. But I knew she was talking about my mom. I felt it. And even then, I was still hoping I was wrong.

POUR IT OUT

As I rushed to my car, tears streamed down my face. My heart was breaking, and I kept crying out to You. I could not understand how months of prayer could go unanswered. I could not understand how You could let this happen, not after everything we had already been through. Not after burying my brother. How were we supposed to bury our mother, too?

My eyes were swollen, my nose running, my voice trembling as I prayed with every ounce of strength I had left, asking You to let this all be a mistake. I begged You to prove my feelings wrong.

But when I pulled into the apartment complex and saw the white van in front, I knew. I still ran inside, hoping, praying, for a different reality. But there were my grandmother, sister, and aunt sitting on the sofa, crying. My mom's lifeless body was there in the room.

I screamed. I stood frozen in disbelief. I could not accept that she was really gone. I had just seen her three days earlier. I kept thinking, *This cannot be real. This is not happening.* There was still so much I needed to say, so much I wanted her to be a part of. I was not ready.

Your Word tells us to trust You with all our hearts and to lean not on our own understanding, but how do I do that in this kind of pain? How do I trust You now?

God, this feels like a nightmare. I keep waiting to wake up, but this is real. And I do not know how to live with that truth. I do not know how to pick up the pieces of a life shattered by grief.

There I was, standing in the middle of it all, numb, broken, and confused. As I held my baby sister, all I could think was, *Not again.* How could we go through this pain all over again?

God, help me. God, help us. You are the only One who will be able to help us get through this. Even when I do not understand You, even when I do not feel You, I still cry out to You, because there is nowhere else to go with this level of pain.

Love,

Ericka

Takeaway

Denial is a protective response, your heart refusing to accept a reality that feels unbearable. It is okay to sit in shock and to keep asking the hard questions. Trust is not erased by doubt; it is a path that can hold both the cry of "Why?" and the slow, fragile steps back toward faith. Be gentle with yourself as you learn to live in the ache.

Scripture (ESV)

Psalm 34:18: "The Lord is near to the brokenhearted and saves the crushed in spirit."

Prayer

Lord, I am stunned and confused. I come to You with a heart that cannot understand and hands that feel empty. Meet me in this disbelief, hold me when I cannot hold myself. Help me trust You when my questions feel louder than my faith. Bring comfort to my family and give us the strength to face what we cannot understand. Even in this darkness, remind me that You are near. Amen.

Denial: Trying to Wake from the Nightmare

Introduction

This letter was written in those first surreal days when I thought, at any moment, I would wake up and find that none of this was real. My mind refused to catch up with my reality.

Letter to God

Dear God,

I keep waiting for someone to shake me awake and tell me this is just a nightmare. Every time my phone rings, I expect it to be her. Every time I send a text, I wait for her reply. I find myself reading her old messages, replaying our conversations over and over in my head.

It is hard to believe that all I have now are memories of her voice, because I will never hear it again. I literally saw her just three days ago. We had Thanksgiving dinner together. I told her I would see her on Saturday so we could go Christmas shopping. And now, here I am on Saturday, making funeral arrangements. This cannot be real. She cannot really be gone forever.

My heart aches with her absence, but my mind will not accept it. I am going through all the funeral checklists, but it is all a blur. Everything feels like a blur.

In the midst of this, I am trying to finish my finals. I am burying my mother during finals week. Nothing on my computer makes sense. I am writing these final papers, but I do not even know if they make sense. I feel like a lost child wandering the streets, desperate for direction.

God, I thought my faith would prepare me for this. I thought loving You meant I could handle anything. But nothing prepared me for the silence after she left. Nothing prepared me for the way my world would tilt and never feel steady again.

I do not know how to live with this truth. Honestly, I do not even know if I want to.

If this is reality, Lord, please hold me. Hold me here until I can breathe again, because right now every breath feels like a battle I am not sure I want to fight.

Love,

Ericka

Takeaway

Denial makes the world look like it is moving on while your soul stands still. It is okay if your head has not yet caught up to your reality.

Scripture (ESV)

Psalm 34:18: "The Lord is near to the brokenhearted and saves the crushed in spirit."

Prayer

Lord, You see my numbness and confusion. You know I am not ready to face the full truth of this loss. Please be patient with me in this space between reality and acceptance. Wrap me in Your nearness until my heart can bear what my mind already knows. Amen.

Denial: When Reality Feels Too Painful to Face

Introduction

This letter was written on the morning of my wedding day, a day that was supposed to be filled with joy, yet all I felt was the weight of absence. The ache of knowing my mother and brother would not be there was unbearable. Denial became my way of surviving what my heart could not yet accept.

Letter to God

Dear God,

As I wake up and prepare for my wedding day, all I feel is sadness and disappointment. I cannot believe I am getting married, and my mother and brother are not here. My mom already had my wedding colors picked out. She would always tell me, "When you get married, I have all the planning under control. All you have to do is show up." We would laugh as I insisted on choosing my own colors, and she would smile and say, "No, I have this."

Now here I am, with tears in my eyes and a shattered heart, wishing that today of all days I could hear her voice and her laugh one more time. I wish my brother could burst into the room to tease me while I get my hair and makeup done. I cannot wrap my head around the reality that I have to experience this milestone with only their memories beside me.

This is not how I imagined things would be. It feels like I am trapped in a bad dream, and I keep waiting for someone to pinch me so I can wake up. Did You not know, God, that I would need my mom for moments like this? Everyone keeps asking if I am excited, and I try to flash a smile, but there is no real joy in my heart right now. I cannot accept this reality.

I have done such a good job keeping myself busy, using the distractions of life to avoid the truth. But today, as I prepare to walk down the aisle, I am forced to face it: my mom is really gone. The pain is indescribable. Inside, I just want to fall to the ground, kick, and scream like a child who does not want to be left behind.

God, I need You to meet me here in this brokenness. I need You to hold me and help me come to terms with what feels unbearable. Please help me make it through this day. I do not want my pain to overshadow this moment. I do not want my husband to feel the weight of my sorrow. Please, Lord, comfort me. Wrap me in Your presence and breathe Your joy into my heart, even in the middle of my grief.

Love,

Ericka

Takeaway

Denial often protects us from pain we are not ready to face. Even when reality feels too heavy to bear, God's presence is steady. He meets us in the ache and gently helps us face what we cannot face alone.

Scripture (ESV)

Psalm 34:18: "The Lord is near to the brokenhearted and saves the crushed in spirit."

Prayer

Lord, this day feels so heavy. My heart aches with the weight of loss, and I do not know how to move forward without the ones I love. Help me feel Your nearness in this moment. Give me the strength to honor their memory with peace instead of despair. Fill the empty spaces in my heart with Your comfort and steady my steps with Your love. Amen.

Denial: When I Pretend I'm Okay

Introduction

This letter came during a season when I had learned how to keep going, smiling, working, and showing up for others, while quietly carrying the ache of grief. I convinced myself I was fine because the tears were not as constant, but deep down, I knew I was still avoiding the pain that never really went away.

Letter to God

Dear God,

I have gotten good at pretending I am okay. I have learned how to smile, laugh, and say "I am fine" when people ask how I am doing. I tell myself I have moved on, but if I am honest, I have only learned how to hide the heaviness better.

There are moments when the grief sneaks up on me—a song, a smell, a photo—and suddenly all the emotions I have pushed down come rushing back. I quickly wipe the tears away before anyone sees. I do not want to be the one still "stuck" in grief while everyone else seems to have moved on.

I have filled my days with busyness, as if staying productive could protect me from feeling the loss. But when the world gets quiet, the sadness creeps back in. I realize I have been trying to outpace grief instead of facing it. I talk about my mom and brother as if I have accepted it, but some part of me still waits for them to walk through the door.

God, I know You see past the smile. You see the part of me that is still numb, still afraid to fully feel. Please help me stop pretending with You. I do not want to keep hiding behind strength that is really just survival. Help me slow down long enough to let You meet me in the pain I have been avoiding.

Teach me that healing does not mean forgetting—that I can honor their memory without losing myself in grief. Let Your presence be the safe place where I can finally be honest about how much this still hurts.

Love,

Ericka

Takeaway

Pretending to be okay can protect us for a season, but true healing begins when we let God into the parts of our grief we have tried to hide. We do not have to hold it all together to be loved. God meets us in the truth of our pain, not in the perfection of our performance.

Scripture (ESV)

Psalm 139:7-8: "Where shall I go from your Spirit? Or where shall I flee from your presence? If I ascend to heaven, you are there! If I make my bed in Sheol, you are there!"

Prayer

Lord, I have been pretending I am okay because it feels safer than admitting I am still hurting. Thank You for seeing beyond my mask and loving me anyway. Help me slow down and face the parts of my grief I have avoided. Meet me with gentleness and remind me that I do not have to hide from You. Amen.

STAGE 2:
Anger

When pain burns hot and questions rise.

Anger doesn't make you faithless-it makes you human. Even in your fury and confusion, God can handle your honesty. He welcomes your cries, your questions, your silence. Every tear and shout is still a prayer He understands.

*I can bring even my anger to God-
He is not afraid of my truth.*

Anger: When My Faith Felt Betrayed

Introduction

This letter came from a place where grief and anger collided. My pain was so deep it felt like betrayal, as if God had turned away when I needed Him most.

Letter to God

Dear God,

I cannot believe You did exactly what I begged You not to do. I asked You not to take my mom. I told You I could not handle losing both my mom and my brother in the same year.

After my brother was murdered, gunned down in the street only minutes after calling my mom to pick up my nephew, she was never the same. I watched her wither under the crushing weight of guilt she did not deserve. That guilt ate her alive, and I was powerless to stop it.

And You watched too. You could have intervened. You could have changed the narrative. I have seen people recover from multiple gunshot wounds. I have seen parents find resilience after losing a child. Why could that not be our story? Why could You not save even one of them?

Now my mom will never see me get married, never hold my children, never help me decorate my first home, or care for me when I am sick. How could You take her from me at twenty-five? The tears will not stop. The ache in my chest feels unbearable.

I have tried to live a holy life. I was not perfect, but I was faithful. I have been mocked for my faith, called the "weird church girl," all for You. And now here I am, writing this letter with disappointment so deep it shakes me.

I have graduate school to finish because You know how much my mom valued education. But how am I supposed to focus? How am I supposed to carry this pain and still show up for life?

I am Your daughter. You were supposed to protect me. You were supposed to love me, not crush me. Please, take this pain away. Wrap me in Your arms. Show me, somehow, that Your grace really is sufficient. Draw near to my broken heart because I cannot do this alone.

Love,

Ericka

Takeaway

Anger in grief does not mean a lack of faith; it means your heart knows God is powerful enough to have done something different. Even when we cannot reconcile the "why," He is still willing to sit with us in the "how."

Scripture (ESV)

Psalm 34:18: "The Lord is near to the brokenhearted and saves the crushed in spirit."

Prayer

Lord, this pain feels unbearable, and my questions feel louder than my faith. I do not understand Your decisions, and my heart is raw with anger and loss. But even here, I am asking You to stay close. Hold me when I cannot hold on to You. Show me that You have not abandoned me in my grief. Amen.

Anger: The Unfairness of It All

Introduction

This letter came from a place where my grief felt sharp, loud, and boiling over. It was a season when my prayers turned into arguments, and I stopped trying to hide how much I did not understand God's choices.

Letter to God

Dear God,

It is not fair. I have said it a hundred times in my head, and now I am saying it to You. It is not fair that other people get miracles and I get memories. It is not fair that You could have stepped in, but You did not.

I have seen You heal strangers. I have heard testimonies of people surviving impossible odds. I have watched parents find strength after burying their children. But when it came to me, to my family, You were silent.

I cannot wrap my mind around it, Lord. You had the power to stop this. You had the power to change the story. Instead, I am left with the ache of what could have been.

Everywhere I turn, I see reminders of what I have lost. And every time I hear someone say, "God is good," I want to ask, But was He good to me? My faith says yes, but my heart does not feel it right now.

I have tried to pray the right prayers, but all I have today are questions. Why them? Why now? Why this way? And maybe worst of all, why me?

I am tired of pretending I understand. I do not. And I do not think I ever will on this side of heaven.

God, I need You to meet me here, in the rawness and in the mess. I need You to remind me that my anger does not disqualify me from Your love.

Because right now, I do not feel holy. I just feel hurt.

Love,

Ericka

Takeaway

God is big enough to handle your anger. He would rather have your honest heart than your quiet resentment.

Scripture (ESV)

Psalm 13:2: "How long must I take counsel in my soul and have sorrow in my heart all the day? How long shall my enemy be exalted over me?"

Prayer

Lord, You know my thoughts before I speak them. You see my anger and still call me Yours. Help me bring even this to You without shame. Meet me in my frustration and show me that You can handle all of me, even the parts I try to hide. Amen.

Anger: Where is the Justice?

Introduction

This letter comes from the kind of fury grief makes, hot, sharp, and honest. It is written from the place where prayers turned into questions, and I stopped pretending to understand how God works.

Letter to God

Dear God,

I am furious. I am angry about what happened to my brother. I am angry that the world moves on while my family still waits for justice. I am angry that he was murdered in broad daylight and there are no witnesses. I am angry that people would rather "mind their own business" than speak up about what they know.

I am angry that my brother has become another statistic, another Black man taken by the streets, and that now he is remembered mostly for how he died instead of how he lived before the streets consumed him. I am angry at a system that moves slowly when lives are urgent. Regardless of the life he chose, he was still ours. He was still loved.

I am angry his case sits on a shelf while his killers walk free. Where is the justice? I am angry that my nephews must grow up without their father. I am angry that I have to watch my mother deteriorate before my eyes. I am angry every time the news brings another story of gun violence and my heart breaks all over again. I am angry that so many families bear this same pain.

How can You be a just God and allow this violence in the world You made? Why are we forced to suffer like this? I know You give people free will, and my brother made choices that led him down a dangerous path. But You could have reached him. He grew up in church, so why did You not convict him, pull him back, or make him want to change? Why did our prayers, our love, our warnings not save him? So many people find God in prison; why was his story not different?

You knew my mother was already fragile. His death made it worse. I am watching her fade, and it hurts me to see her suffering. I am angry that You are allowing me to feel this depth of pain.

I want justice. I am tired of pretending I am okay with what happened. I am not okay. This is not fair. I deserved better. My mom deserved better. My family deserved better.

Please help me. I feel like I am drowning. I do not want to become a person rooted in rage. I do not want to drift away from You. Right now, I do not feel connected, I feel abandoned, and I need You to sit with me in this rage and this sorrow. I need to feel You. I need help to reconcile these thoughts and emotions. Help me see through Your eyes. Honor my honesty and help me make sense of this.

I cannot keep carrying this anger. It is changing me and how I show up. Help me transform my mind and mend my broken heart. Help my family find justice, help my mother find relief, and help my nephews grow with love and protection.

Love,

Ericka

Takeaway

Say the hard things. God can take your anger and your honesty; He would rather have your raw, aching truth than a quiet, false peace. Justice, healing, and transformation can begin where you are honest.

Scripture (ESV)

Habakkuk 1:2-4: "O LORD, how long shall I cry for help, and you will not hear? Or cry to you, 'Violence!' and you will not save? ... Why do you make me see iniquity, and why do you idly look at wrong? ... The law is paralyzed, and justice never goes forth."

Prayer

Lord, I bring You my anger and my questions. You see the injustice, the loss, and the family that is breaking. Meet us in this pain. Give us justice where justice is due, comfort for my mother, protection for my nephews, and clarity for my heart. Do not punish my honesty; use it to heal me. Teach me how to carry this grief without letting it harden me. Hold us, mend us, and lead us toward truth and restoration. Amen.

Anger: When I Felt Forgotten

Introduction

This letter poured out during a season when grief collided with exhaustion. I was trying to hold everything together—wife, mother, professional—while quietly breaking under the weight of missing my mom and brother. Everywhere I looked, I saw reminders of what I did not have, and it felt as if God had turned His face away.

Letter to God

Dear God,

I am so disappointed in You. When will the pain and suffering end? I feel like I am drowning. Not only did You take my mom, but You took her before my children ever had the chance to meet her.

Now here I am, trying to balance life, grief, and motherhood while supporting my husband through his hectic work schedule, and I feel so alone. I watch other people call their moms for help, see grandmothers picking up their grandkids from school or taking them to the park. I even see them laughing together at the grocery store. And every time, my heart aches.

I long for my mother's help. I rush from work to pick up my kids, manage grocery shopping and toddler meltdowns, and try to hold it all together. My husband is doing what he is supposed to do, providing for our family, but I cannot understand why You have allowed others to have the very support I need most.

My dad and bonus mom are wonderful when they visit, but even then, You did not consider me enough to let them live close by. This is not how my life was supposed to be. My mother was supposed to be here. My children were supposed to know her laugh, her warmth, her wisdom. They were supposed to have their uncle, my brother, to joke with and learn from.

I feel so cheated by You. I feel betrayed. It makes me angry, bitter even. I deserved to share these milestones with my mom and brother. Being surrounded by people who have what I have lost feels like You are taunting me.

Why would You allow this kind of heartbreak? Why would You let me sit in this kind of emptiness? I cannot understand. But here I am, still sitting at Your feet, desperate for answers. Here I am, feeling betrayed by the One I thought loved me the most. Here I am, clinging to what little hope I have left.

If You can hear me, if You are still listening, I need You. I need You to help me reconcile this pain. I do not want to walk around with this anger anymore. I do not want my heart to tighten every time I see another woman experiencing the joy and support I crave. Please, God, take this bitterness away. Remind me that You are still a God who can love me through even this.

Love,

Ericka

Takeaway

Grief often carries hidden anger, not because we have lost faith, but because our hearts ache for the love and support we once knew. Even when we feel forgotten, God's love still finds its way into the cracks of our pain.

Scripture (ESV)

Psalm 13:1-2: "How long, O Lord? Will you forget me forever?
How long will you hide your face from me?
How long must I take counsel in my soul and have sorrow in my heart all the day?"

Prayer

Lord, I do not understand why this had to happen. The ache feels endless, and anger sits heavy in my chest. I miss my mom. I miss my brother. I miss the version of life I thought I would have. Please meet me here, in my frustration and confusion. Teach me that Your presence is not dependent on my understanding. Remind me that You are still near, even when I feel abandoned. Amen.

Anger: When I Feel Like I'm Failing

Introduction

This letter came from a season when grief felt heavy on top of life's demands. I was juggling motherhood, marriage, work, and the weight of loss, and it felt as if I was failing at everything, including myself.

Letter to God

Dear God,

I am so frustrated with myself. I cannot seem to get it right. I cannot seem to handle all the responsibilities on my plate while carrying this grief. I try to be patient with my children, loving with my husband, and diligent at work, but I keep falling short.

I get angry at myself for feeling tired or overwhelmed. I get angry that I cry over small things or snap at the people I love. I wish I could hold it all together the way I imagine others do. I feel like I am letting everyone down, my children, my husband, even You.

I finally developed enough strength to seek grief counseling, thinking it would help me process this pain so I could perform better, manage my life more efficiently, and be the mom, wife, and daughter You want me to be. But instead, it has felt like I am reliving everything all over again. Every session opens wounds I thought I had tucked away. I leave feeling heavier, more raw, and even more frustrated with myself for not being "better" yet.

I resent that trying to do the right thing, trying to heal, only seems to make the ache more vivid. I resent that my heart still aches so deeply for my mom and my brother. I feel inadequate. I feel angry. I feel defeated.

Yet here I am, still seeking You. I need You to remind me that being human does not mean I am failing. I need You to teach me that grief and weakness do not disqualify me from love, purpose, or Your care. Help me forgive myself when I stumble. Help me see that even when seeking help feels painful, it is still part of the journey You have for me.

Love,

Ericka

Takeaway

Seeking help does not always make grief easier; sometimes it intensifies it. But opening ourselves to support and processing pain is a step toward healing, even when it feels uncomfortable. God is present in both the relief and the discomfort, meeting us in our weakness.

Scripture (ESV)

2 Corinthians 12:9: "But he said to me, 'My grace is sufficient for you, for my power is made perfect in weakness.' Therefore I will boast all the more gladly of my weaknesses, so that the power of Christ may rest upon me."

Prayer

Lord, I am tired and frustrated with myself. I sought help, expecting relief, and instead felt my grief all over again. Teach me to trust that even when healing feels painful, You are guiding me. Help me forgive myself and embrace Your grace in my weakness. Amen.

STAGE 3:
Bargaining

When you wish for what could have been.

You replay moments, make promises, and search for another way the story could have gone. In this reaching, God doesn't scold - He listens. He teaches surrender not as defeat, but as rest for your weary heart.

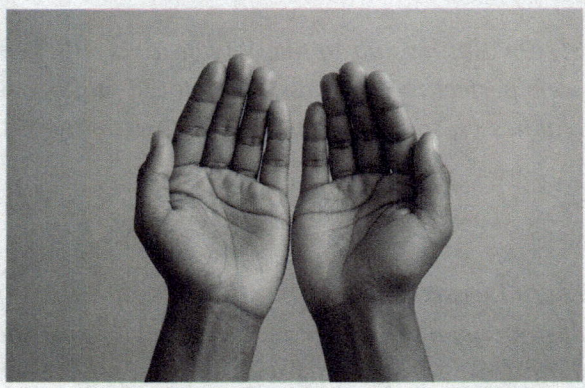

*I release what I cannot rewrite
and rest in God's care.*

Bargaining: When I Begged to Trade Places

Introduction

This letter comes from the raw, bargaining place of grief, where desperation looks for any trade, promise, or plea that might change a terrible outcome. It is an honest, aching attempt to make a deal with God to keep the person you need most.

Letter to God

Dear God,

Please do not take her. I will do whatever You ask of me. We need each other to get through this. My brother just died; I cannot handle losing my mother, too. She has two other children who need her. God, You cannot let her be taken from us in the same year. That is too much. It is unthinkable.

I am in graduate school, trying my best to push through this unbearable pain. My nephew needs my mom. He is too young to lose his grandmother right after losing his dad. That kind of pain would crush him. He does not deserve it.

God, I know You hear me. I know our days are already numbered in Your plan. But I am begging You—this depression is consuming my mother. I do not even recognize her anymore. Some days, I cannot answer the phone because it hurts too much to hear the agony in her voice. I am losing her. She is giving up. I can feel it. I can see it.

Please, God. Help her. Heal her. For me, for my sister, and for my nephews. There is still so much left for us to experience together. She has to see me graduate with my master's degree. She has to see me marry Brandon and watch me become a mother. She has to see Destiny graduate from college. She has to help me decorate my first home.

I need her. I miss her, the version of her that existed before my brother was murdered. Please do not take her from me. My heart cannot take it. My sister cannot take it.

Your Word says You are close to the brokenhearted. So here I am, my heart shattered into a million pieces. I am crying out to You from a place of desperation. I feel like I am drowning in pain and sorrow. I do not know how much longer I can pretend to be okay.

Please, God. I need You.

Love,

Ericka

Takeaway

Bargaining in grief is not weakness; it is the human heart trying to regain control when everything feels stolen. Promises and pleas do not negate faith—they show how much we depend on God's presence and intervention in our loss. Even when God does not change the outcome, He can still meet us in the middle of our bargaining, carrying us, steadying us, and holding the pieces we cannot hold ourselves.

Scripture (ESV)

Psalm 34:18: "The Lord is near to the brokenhearted and saves the crushed in spirit."

Prayer

Lord, I come to You desperate and bargaining from a place of deep pain. My heart is torn, and I do not know how to hold all of this grief. Please come near to my mother and to our family. Bring healing where there is despair, strength where there is giving up, and hope where we cannot see a way forward. Help me trust You even when I do not understand. Hold us close and carry us through. Amen.

Bargaining: When Every Prayer Pleads for a Different Ending

Introduction

This letter comes from the raw bargaining place where grief and hope collide—when you are willing to trade everything for one more day, one more breath, one more miracle. Bargaining is not weakness; it is your heart still reaching for God, testing the edges of faith for evidence that He hears and moves.

Letter to God

Dear God,

I do not know who You think I am, or what You see when You look at me that makes You believe I can handle another hardship.

As I sit in the ICU with my grandmother, unsure if she will live or die, all I can do is beg and cry. Please do not take my granny. I am literally in the middle of grief counseling for the deaths of my mom and my brother. I have finally mustered the courage to sit with these wounds, and I am doing it in partnership with You. I am not leaving You out of the process. Does that not count for something?

Please tell me You see how hard I am trying to be a better daughter and a better woman, to grow, to heal, to bring You glory through it all. Please heal my granny. Her blood pressure is dangerously high. They are saying she will need dialysis, and she is telling me she does not want it. She just made me her health care surrogate. God, I cannot carry this. Not right now. My heart is so raw. This EMDR therapy has left me wide open.

Sitting in this hospital room, anxiety is crushing my chest. The thought of losing her, of planning another funeral, makes me sick. Every time I ask her a question about end-of-life wishes, my head throbs. My spirit trembles. I just do not understand—what more do You want from me? If You tell me, I will do it. I am praying daily. I have found a church home. I am back in Your house. I am trying so hard to repair our relationship. And I have finally reached a place where I have released my anger, where I have forgiven You for taking my mom and my brother. So please, do not take me back there. Not again. Not now.

Show me that Your Word still holds power. Show me that the God who healed the woman with the issue of blood, the God who raised the man at the pool of Bethesda, still lives, still moves, still heals. I am writing to that God, and I am asking You to use that same healing power to touch my granny in this ICU bed. She has already endured so much loss. She deserves peace. We deserve some peace. Please, let this story end differently. Let at least one of our stories have a happy ending. Please, Father. Please. Heal her.

Love always,

Ericka

Takeaway

Bargaining is the honest work of a heart trying to make sense of what feels senseless. It is not a failure of faith—it is proof you still believe God can intervene. Bring your offers, your bargains, your promises, and your raw pleading to Him. Prayer is not a transaction; it is relationship. Even when the answer is not what you hope, your prayers matter and shape the way you move into the next chapter.

Scripture (ESV)

James 5:15: "And the prayer of faith will save the one who is sick, and the Lord will raise him up. And if he has committed sins, he will be forgiven."

Prayer

Father, my hands are empty and my heart is overflowing. I bring my granny before You now—her frailty, her fear, her tiredness. If it is Your will, heal her by Your powerful hand. Comfort her, steady the doctors, give wisdom to every decision, and surround our family with Your peace that surpasses understanding. If healing looks different from what I hope, carry us through it, and make Your presence unmistakable in the middle of our ache. Help me keep trusting You even when I do not understand. Amen.

Bargaining: God, Give Me Just One More Day

Introduction

This letter came from a place of desperation, where I was willing to give anything, change anything, be anything, if it meant I could have her back for just one more day.

Letter to God

Dear God,

If I could have just one more day with her, I would make it count. I would not waste a second. I would pick up the phone when she called. I would let her vent all she wanted about my brother's death. I would make space for her grief. I would tell her I love her and make sure she understood how much I meant it.

God, I am begging You—just one day. I will do anything You ask of me. I will give up every comfort I have, I will carry whatever weight You place on my shoulders, if You would only let me see her again.

I keep replaying our last conversation, wondering if I missed a sign, wondering if I should have stayed longer, asked one more question, hugged her one more time. If You gave me another chance, I would fix every moment I got wrong.

It is hard to believe my days with her are over when my heart still has so much left to give. So many things I did not say. So many ways I could have loved her better.

God, I know You cannot be bribed. I know time is in Your hands alone. But still, my heart whispers, Maybe if I promise enough, maybe if I pray hard enough…

I am clinging to You in this place between hope and heartbreak. I am asking, pleading, for a miracle that defies the rules of this life.

One more dinner date.

One more phone call.

One more laugh.

One more hug.

Just one more day, Lord. Please.

Love,

Ericka

Takeaway

Bargaining is the desperate attempt to undo the unchangeable. God hears even these prayers—the ones that sound like pleading bargains instead of polished faith.

Scripture (ESV)

Psalm 39:4: "O Lord, make me know my end and what is the measure of my days; let me know how fleeting I am!"

Prayer

Lord, You know the longing that keeps me awake at night. You see the ache that makes me wish for another yesterday. Help me trust You in the places I cannot control and teach me to rest in the truth that You waste nothing, not even my deepest longing. Amen.

Bargaining: When I Try to Earn My Healing

Introduction

This letter came from a season when I thought that if I kept giving, serving, and showing up for others, God might take away my pain. I poured myself out, hoping my sacrifice would somehow be enough to exchange my grief for joy. But the more I gave, the emptier I felt.

Letter to God

Dear God,

I have been trying so hard to fix this ache inside me. I convinced myself that if I kept serving others, if I kept being strong, maybe You would take this grief away. I have stretched myself thin, saying yes to every need, every request, every opportunity to help—hoping that my faithfulness might earn me some relief.

I thought if I kept moving, kept loving, kept giving, You would see my effort and bless me with joy again. Instead, I feel exhausted. I feel unseen. And underneath it all, I am still grieving.

God, I realize now that my overextending was not just generosity—it was a bargain. A silent plea: If I keep doing good, will You please take this pain away? I do not know how to simply sit with You in my brokenness. I do not know how to believe that I could be loved even when I had nothing left to give.

I keep trying to earn what You have already promised me—Your presence, Your peace, Your love. But I cannot trade my exhaustion for healing, can I? I cannot perform my way into wholeness.

Lord, I need You to help me rest in grace instead of striving for relief. Teach me that joy is not a reward for overworking, it is a gift that flows from surrender. I do not want to serve out of desperation anymore; I want to serve out of overflow. Fill the parts of me I have emptied, trying to prove that I am okay.

Love,

Ericka

Takeaway

Sometimes our service becomes a silent bargain—we give, hoping God will remove our pain in return. But healing is not earned; it is received. God restores joy not through striving but through surrender and stillness in His presence.

Scripture (ESV)

Matthew 11:28-30: "Come to me, all who labor and are heavy laden, and I will give you rest. Take my yoke upon you, and learn from me, for I am gentle and lowly in heart, and you will find rest for your souls. For my yoke is easy, and my burden is light."

Prayer

Lord, I have been trying to work my way into healing, believing my sacrifice could earn me peace. Forgive me for confusing service with surrender. Teach me to rest in Your grace and receive joy as the gift it is, not the reward I must chase. Help me serve from a full heart, not an empty one. Amen.

Bargaining: When I Stop Trying to Make It Make Sense

Introduction

This letter came from the moment I realized I had spent so much time trying to make sense of my loss. I wanted to believe that if I endured with grace, if I served with purpose, if I showed strength through my pain, then maybe God would make it all feel worth it. Over time, I learned that healing is not a transaction, and purpose does not erase grief. Only when I stopped trying to fix the pain did I finally begin to feel peace.

Letter to God

Dear God,

I have spent so much time trying to find meaning in this pain. I told myself that if I could just understand why You allowed it, maybe I could accept it. I tried to make the loss make sense, to turn my grief into something purposeful so it would not feel so heavy.

I thought that if I kept showing up strong, serving others, and turning my sorrow into ministry, You would trade my pain for peace. I believed that if I could find the lesson in all of this, the ache would go away. But the truth is, no purpose can replace the people I have lost. No amount of meaning makes their absence easier to carry.

I have prayed, cried, and reasoned with You, trying to make this story line up neatly with Your promises. I am starting to realize that maybe You were never asking me to make sense of it. Maybe You were asking me to trust You even when it does not make sense.

God, I am tired of trying to fix what only You can heal. I am tired of negotiating with pain, tired of performing peace I do not yet feel. I want to rest now. I want to stop trying to earn the comfort You freely offer.

Help me stop demanding that this loss be useful just to justify its pain. Teach me that Your goodness is not proven by my understanding, it is proven by Your presence. I do not need all the answers to believe You are still here. I do not need to find purpose to find peace. I just need You.

Love,

Ericka

Takeaway

We often bargain with God, hoping He will make the pain meaningful so it feels worth enduring. True peace comes not from finding purpose in loss but from trusting His presence within it. Healing begins when we stop trying to make sense of what happened and allow God to hold us in it.

Scripture (ESV)

Proverbs 3:5-6: "Trust in the Lord with all your heart, and do not lean on your own understanding. In all your ways acknowledge him, and he will make straight your paths."

Prayer

Lord, I have spent so long trying to make this pain make sense, trying to trade my faithfulness for understanding. Help me let go of that need. Teach me to rest in the mystery of Your goodness, even when I do not have answers. Let peace rise where striving once lived. Meet me in surrender, and help me trust that You are still working, even here. Amen.

STAGE 4:
Depression

When sorrow feels endless.
You feel the weight of it all – the quiet,
the ache, the absence. But even here, in
the dim light of grief, God does not leave.
He sits beside you in the stillness,
holding space for your pain until
you can breathe again.

Even in darkness, I am not
alone. God's presence is my
comfort.

Depression: When Grief Feels Like a Heavy Blanket

Introduction

This letter comes from the deep, sinking place of grief where everything feels muted and moving is an act of bravery. Depression after loss can look like apathy, exhaustion, and a thick, isolating fog, and every small task becomes a mountain.

Letter to God

Dear God,

I am struggling to get out of bed. I do not care about anything anymore. I feel numb. I feel defeated. I feel hopeless.

There is so much I should be doing—homework, overdue notes for work, cleaning my house—but I cannot bring myself to do any of it. I feel like I am falling apart. I have tried so hard to avoid thinking about the grief, but today I had a moment when I wanted to call my mom, and then I remembered I cannot.

The realization hit me like a ton of bricks, and all I could do was weep. O God, this pain is unbearable. It hurts so deeply. All I want to do is sleep so I do not have to feel anything at all. I cannot see the light at the end of this tunnel. I cannot even imagine how You could heal this kind of pain. It feels impossible.

Right now, it feels like I will never get through this. Grief is consuming me. What makes it even worse is that it is not just my mom—you took my brother, too. The pain of losing them both leaves me breathless. My spirit feels crushed. My life will never be the same.

It is hard to picture myself on the other side of this. The thought that I might feel this broken forever is overwhelming.

So, God, I am praying. I am praying for comfort. I am praying for strength. I am praying for hope. I am praying for the ability to see beyond this sorrow, because right now, sorrow is all I know.

My faith feels weak. My hope feels gone. But I am still asking—please restore me. Please wrap me in Your arms. I need to feel Your love, God. I need to know that Your love is strong enough to carry me through this dark season.

I need You.

Love,

Ericka

Takeaway

Depression in grief is not a moral failing; it is an understandable response to profound loss. When motivation disappears and days blend together, the smallest acts of self-care become courageous steps forward. You do not have to see the whole path; you only need to take the next small step and let God walk beside you through the darkness.

Scripture (ESV)

Psalm 34:18: "The Lord is near to the brokenhearted and saves the crushed in spirit."

Prayer

Lord, the weight of this grief is crushing, and I feel hollowed out by sorrow. Come near to me in this dark season. Hold me when I cannot hold myself. Give me strength for one small task, courage to reach out when I am alone, and hope to believe there will be mornings when the fog lifts. Restore my soul, even in small pieces, and remind me that I am not abandoned. Amen.

Depression: When a Milestone Feels Hollow

Introduction

This letter comes from the hollow ache of reaching a milestone without the one who championed you. Graduation should feel triumphant, and it can, but grief often arrives in the doorway of our greatest victories. That does not make your achievement any less real; it simply means celebration and sorrow can sit together for a time.

Letter to God

Dear God,

Today is graduation day. I am receiving my Master of Social Work degree—something I worked so hard for, something my mother was so proud of. I should be feeling joy. I should be smiling. But all I feel is anguish and pain.

This is my first major milestone without her. She was so passionate about education. As a first-generation college graduate, she beamed with pride when I told her I was going to grad school. She had already picked the perfect spot to hang my degree. I used to love watching the pride light up her eyes. She worked so hard to care for us, and I cherished every opportunity to show her that her sacrifices were not in vain.

God, she was supposed to be here today—helping me get ready, fussing over the little details, capturing every moment. Instead, I am left with a decorated cap bearing her photo and the words, "How is the view from heaven, Mom?" This does not feel fair. No one prepares you for life without a parent, especially not for moments like this. As I sit in my room crying, all I can ask is, Why me? Why this kind of pain?

When I walked across the stage, I imagined her screaming my name from the crowd. I watched my peers embrace their mothers after the ceremony, and my heart broke. All I wanted was to hug her one more time and hear her say those words again: "Baby, I am so proud of you." I was surrounded by people ready to celebrate me, yet I felt completely alone. No one truly sees how hard it is to be fully present in this moment. No one talks about how every new milestone can reopen the wounds of grief.

Today was full of I wish and If only Mom and my brother were here. And God, this is just the beginning—the first of many milestones without her. I am really trying to understand the lesson or wisdom I am meant to gain in this season, but right now, all I feel is hopelessness, sorrow, and loneliness.

Please, Lord, let Your love be a blanket wrapped around me. Let Your strength be made perfect in my weakness. Let joy rise up in me today. Do not let grief steal this moment. Do not let sadness and despair overshadow what You have brought me through. God, I need You.

Love,

Ericka

Takeaway

Milestones will not always feel like triumphs—and that is okay. Grief can sit in the same seat as celebration. Give yourself permission to feel both: honor your sorrow and still acknowledge your accomplishment. Let small acts—a call, a photo, a moment of gratitude—be the gentle bridge from pain toward joy. Redemption often arrives one quiet step at a time.

Scripture (ESV)

Psalm 34:18: "The Lord is near to the brokenhearted and saves the crushed in spirit."

Prayer

Lord, today is supposed to be a day of joy, but my heart aches with loss. Wrap me in Your comfort and help me carry both the grief and the gratitude. Give me the courage to celebrate what I have achieved even as I mourn what is missing. Let Your presence fill the empty seats and Your peace settle in my chest. Remind me that my accomplishment matters and that You are with me in every step forward. Amen.

Depression: When Motherhood Meets Grief

Introduction

This letter comes from the tender collision of beginnings and endings, when the joy of new motherhood is shadowed by the grief of losing the mother you wish could still guide you. Depression in this season is more than sadness; it is the ache of longing for comfort that feels irreplaceable.

Letter to God

Dear God,

I want my mom.

This is not how my life was supposed to turn out. Here I am, holding my newborn daughter, and my mother is not here to help me.

I used to laugh and joke with her, saying, "When I have a baby, you are staying with me the entire six weeks of maternity leave." She would always reply, "Girl, whatever," but we both knew she would come. We both knew she would be here.

Yet here I am at home with my one-week-old baby girl, and my mom is not here. I cannot call her. She will never get to hold my daughter. She was not there to help me push or to say, "You got this." My heart is broken.

How am I supposed to manage this stage of my life? How do I grieve the loss of my mother while learning how to be one? I have never experienced pain like this before. As I look into my daughter's eyes, I now understand the depth of a mother's love. Instead of comforting me, that revelation shatters me. Because now that I finally understand what my mother gave me, I cannot tell her. I cannot thank her. I cannot call her and say, "Now I get it."

Becoming a mother has made me even more grateful for the way she loved me—for the sacrifices she made, for the ways she showed up. And now I ache because she is not here for me to say, "Mom, I see you more clearly now."

God, why would You take her before I had the chance to say all of this? Who am I supposed to call when my daughter will not stop crying? Who is going to come over so I can take a nap or a shower? I do not have anyone local to fill that role.

So here I am, holding my baby with tears running down my face. My heart aches so deeply it feels like it is breaking out of my chest. I do not want to get out of bed, but I have to. My daughter is the only thing that keeps me going.

I do not understand Your ways. Please, either help me understand or take this pain away. It is unbearable, Lord, and I do not want my daughter to see how broken her mother really is.

God, I need You. Please help me find some joy in the midst of this pain.

Love always,

Ericka

Takeaway

Grief often shows up strongest at new beginnings because milestones highlight who is missing. It is okay to ache while you celebrate, to long for comfort while you parent. God does not expect you to be unbreakable—He promises to be your strength when you cannot be strong on your own.

Scripture (ESV)

Isaiah 66:13: "As one whom his mother comforts, so I will comfort you; you shall be comforted in Jerusalem."

Prayer

Lord, I am overwhelmed by grief and weariness. I miss my mother more than words can say. In this season when I should be celebrating new life, I am also grieving a deep loss. Help me hold both things at once. Surround me with Your presence and wrap me in comfort only You can give. Be the strength I do not have, the peace I cannot find, and the help I cannot reach.

Help me parent through the pain without pretending it does not exist. Let my daughter see not a perfect mother but a present one—a mother held together by grace. Restore my joy, little by little. Remind me that I am not alone. And somehow, please help me feel my mom's love through the love You continue to pour into me. In Jesus' name I pray, Amen.

Depression: The Days I Could Not Get Out of Bed

Introduction

This letter came from a season when simply existing felt like more than I could handle. I was not living; I was surviving minute to minute, breath to breath.

Letter to God

Dear God,

The bed feels like the only safe place I have left. Even then, it does not really feel safe—just still. No one can see me breaking here. No one can ask me to smile.

I used to wake up with a list of things to do. Now I wake up and wonder if I have the strength to even stand. I hear the world moving outside my window—cars passing, people laughing—but it is like I am trapped behind glass, watching life go on without me.

God, I am so tired. Tired in my bones, in my soul. I do not care about anything anymore—not work, not food, not even the things that used to bring me joy. I cannot remember the last time I laughed from a real place.

I want to pray, but the words get stuck somewhere between my mind and my lips. And when I try to worship, it feels like I am singing into the void. My faith tells me You are here, but my heart feels nothing but silence.

The hardest part, Lord, is that I do not even want to get better today. I just want to disappear into the blankets and not be asked to carry anything— not even myself.

But still, here I am, whispering to You from under the covers. I do not have eloquent words. I do not have bold faith today. I just have this small, desperate prayer:

Please hold me until the light feels possible again.
Love,
Ericka

Takeaway

Depression can make your world feel impossibly small. Even in the smallest spaces, God's presence can fill the room.

Scripture (ESV)

Psalm 42:11: "Why are you cast down, O my soul, and why are you in turmoil within me? Hope in God; for I shall again praise him, my salvation and my God."

Prayer

Lord, I feel trapped in my own body, unable to move forward. I do not have the strength to change today, but I trust that You can carry me through it. Sit with me in this dark place and let Your presence be the one thing I can still feel. Amen.

Depression: The Weight of Guilt

Introduction

This letter comes from the heavy, slow place where guilt and grief sit together—the part of sorrow that whispers you could have done more.

Letter to God

Dear God,

This guilt is consuming me. I keep thinking I should have done more. I should have answered more calls. Maybe if I had been more present, more supportive, my mom would still be here.

There were so many times she called and I did not pick up. Not because I did not love her, but because I could not bear the pain in her voice. I could not stand the way she clung to my brother's case. Every "I talked to the detective—no leads" felt like another knife in my chest. I was trying to hold myself together, and hearing her desperation made me fall apart.

When I visited, she did not look like herself. She felt like a shell of the woman who raised me. She was slipping away right in front of me. What was I supposed to do with that? The only thing I knew how to do was step back. I started calling less. Daily check-ins became three or four times a week. When she texted about my brother, I changed the subject. I just could not handle it.

Now the guilt is eating me alive. My mom tried to share her pain, and I shut her down. I did not give her space to grieve. I put limits on her sorrow and expected her to carry it neatly. How could I do that? Was I really that selfish?

Maybe I was overwhelmed. Grief makes you feel like you are drowning. I was in grad school, working for DCF, doing an internship, barely holding myself together. I thought I was doing the best I could, but now I question everything. I buried my own pain to survive, and talking to my mom only unearthed what I was trying to suppress.

Now I sit haunted by the calls I did not answer and the messages I left unread. God, that hurts. Mom, I am so sorry for all the ways I did not show up when you needed me most.

This pain, coupled with guilt, feels unbearable. Just when I think I have reached the limit, the guilt cuts deeper. People say, "Grief is a journey." God, I want to get off this train. I want to quit. I want to bury this grief and never feel it again.

Healing is hard. It requires more strength than I feel I have. But here I am, still showing up, still talking to You. Because even in this pain, I know I need You.

Please, God, sit with me in this grief and this guilt. I cannot do this without You. I need You.

Love,

Ericka

Takeaway

Guilt is a stubborn shadow, but it does not cancel the love you gave. Apologize, repair where you can, and let grace do the work you cannot. Showing up now matters—not the tally of missed calls.

Scripture (ESV)

Psalm 34:18: "The LORD is near to the brokenhearted and saves the crushed in spirit."

Prayer

Lord, I bring You this heavy guilt and this aching sorrow. You know every missed call and unread message. Help me find mercy for myself and the

POUR IT OUT

courage to make small repairs where I can. Meet my mother's memory and my heart with Your nearness. Teach me how to grieve without letting guilt destroy me. Hold me, heal me, and remind me that Your grace is bigger than my mistakes. Amen.

STAGE 5:

Acceptance

When peace begins to whisper again.

This is not forgetting, and it's not moving on—
it's moving with grace. Acceptance comes
softly, teaching you that love and loss can coexist.
God walks with you into a new day, reminding
you that healing doesn't erase love - it honors it.

I carry both love and loss with peace.
God makes beauty out of what remains.

Acceptance: When Peace Begins to Bloom

Introduction

This letter comes from the place of healing where grief no longer feels like an open wound but like a scar, tender yet carried with honor. Acceptance does not mean the pain disappears; it means you have found peace in carrying both the love and the loss together.

Letter to God

Dear God,

You are so amazing. Today I had the opportunity to minister to someone about how You carried me through my season of grief. As I spoke, I realized how intentional Your love has been, even in the depths of my sorrow.

I shared the story of how I found out I was pregnant on my first Mother's Day without my mom, and how, in the same month of her passing, just weeks after her first death anniversary, my daughter was born. It is surreal to be standing on the other side of grief now. With clarity, I can finally see how Your hand was always on my life. You never left me.

In every moment of pain, anger, and even resentment, You were still comforting me. You were still caring for me. You remained faithful when I could not see past my heartbreak.

Now that I am a mother, my perspective has changed completely. For the longest time, I was angry with my mom. I felt like she gave up on us. I thought she should have fought harder through her own grief. Now I understand. I admire her strength. I see the fight she had. I cannot imagine the pain of having to bury your child, especially a child taken by violence. I cannot imagine what it was like for her to carry that kind of sorrow every single day.

I was so focused on trying to save her that I did not recognize the energy it took for her to keep saving herself. Now I thank You for giving me a new perspective, for softening my heart, and for helping me see her humanity. I am grateful that she no longer feels that pain. I still miss her every day, but now I have peace knowing that her suffering is over. Her sorrow is no more.

Thank You for allowing me to experience this full circle moment. Her legacy did not end on December 2, 2015. Her story lives on through me, and that brings me comfort. It brings me joy. The privilege of honoring her with my life is a gift I am finally learning to appreciate.

I see her in so many of the things I do. She lives on in me.

For the first time, I can say this with honesty: I have peace with her transition. I have peace in my heart, and that peace feels like healing. That peace feels like freedom.

My heart is full of gratitude and admiration. God, I thank You.

Love always,

Ericka

Takeaway

Acceptance is not about forgetting; it is about embracing both the love and the loss with gratitude. When peace begins to replace anguish, grief transforms into legacy, and the memory of our loved ones becomes a source of strength rather than only sorrow.

Scripture (ESV)

Philippians 4:7: "And the peace of God, which surpasses all understanding, will guard your hearts and your minds in Christ Jesus."

Prayer

Lord, thank You for carrying me through the storm and bringing me into a place of peace. Thank You for softening my heart, shifting my perspec-

tive, and helping me honor my mother's legacy with gratitude. Continue to guide me as I walk forward, living with joy, healing, and freedom. May Your peace keep shaping me into a testimony of Your love. Amen.

Acceptance: When Perspective Turns to Gratitude

Introduction

This letter comes from the place where grief shifts into clarity, where the pain no longer overshadows the love, and the loss is reframed through the lens of legacy. Acceptance does not erase the sorrow, but it makes room for gratitude and new meaning to grow.

Letter to God

Dear God,

I am in awe of the way You love me. For the first time in a long time, I can see the light at the end of the tunnel. I have come to realize that my brother's murder was never part of Your divine plan. As I fought my way through the darkness of grief, You continued to show me how all things are still working together, even in pain.

There was a time when every thought of my brother's death overwhelmed me with anger and sorrow. Now, when I reflect on his passing, I see the courage and love that defined his final moments. My nephew was with him just before he was killed. When my brother learned that the men who wanted to harm him were nearby, he called my mom to pick up my nephew.

For so long, I wrestled with that moment, angry with You, God. I could not understand why You did not save my brother. I kept asking why he did not get in the car with my mom and nephew. I thought that if he had, everything would still be fine.

But the truth is, if my brother had gotten in that car, I might have lost more than just him on February 28, 2015.

He stayed behind to protect them. He fought long enough to make sure his son and our mother were not caught in the crossfire. He ensured they were safe. I cannot begin to imagine the courage it took to make that decision, to stand in the face of danger, to say goodbye to his son, knowing it would be the last time. That was an act of unconditional love.

Now, when I think about my brother's story, I see him not as a victim but as a hero. I see the way You honored his final prayer, to keep his son safe. Thank You for giving me a new perspective. Thank You for covering and protecting my mom and nephew that day.

Now, ten years later, that same nephew lives with me. That is how I know You are real. Parenting and nurturing my brother's son has been both healing and redemptive. It feels like a piece of my brother lives on with me. I have had the privilege of witnessing proud parent moments on his behalf, and that fills my heart with joy.

Watching my nephews grow has been one of the most rewarding parts of my life. In them, I see my brother's legacy, his brilliance, his motivation, and his entrepreneurial spirit. His potential did not die with him. It lives on.

God, I thank You for giving me what I needed, even when I did not have the words to ask for it. I did not know how to pray for this, but You heard the cries of my heart. For that, I am eternally grateful.

Thank You for loving me with such intentionality and compassion. I love You.

Love, Your grateful daughter,

Ericka

Takeaway

Acceptance allows us to see loss not only through the lens of sorrow but also through the lens of legacy. The story does not end at the grave; it continues in the love, courage, and life left behind. Gratitude grows when we recognize how God redeems even the darkest chapters.

Scripture (ESV)

Romans 8:28: "And we know that for those who love God all things work together for good, for those who are called according to his purpose."

Prayer

Lord, thank You for redeeming my pain and transforming my perspective. Thank You for showing me the courage in my brother's sacrifice and for keeping his legacy alive through his children. Help me continue honoring his memory with gratitude instead of anger. May I never forget that even in grief, Your love remains intentional, faithful, and unshakable. Amen.

Acceptance: Her Legacy Lives Through Me

Introduction

This letter came from the first moment I realized that my grief was not only about what I had lost, but also about what I still carried from her life.

Letter to God

Dear God,

I used to think acceptance meant being okay with what happened. I thought it meant I had to stop missing her or stop wishing she were here. Now I understand, acceptance is knowing she is gone and still finding ways to keep her with me.

I see her in my smile when I am proud of something. I hear her in the way I encourage others. I feel her in the quiet strength I did not know I had until I had to survive without her.

Her lessons did not die with her. Her love did not die with her. Every prayer she ever prayed over me is still alive, still working.

God, I used to be afraid that time would erase her from my life, that one day her voice would fade from my memory, or I would forget the sound of her laugh. You have shown me that her presence is woven into me, into my habits, my values, my words.

Every time I choose kindness when it is hard, that is her. Every time I fight for someone else's dignity, that is her. Every time I love deeply and unapologetically, that is her. Every time I speak my mind without apology, that is her.

Her legacy lives in me because You chose her to be my mother. For that, Lord, I am grateful, even through the ache. I may never stop missing her, but I am learning to live in a way that makes her proud. Somehow, that brings me peace.

Love,

Ericka

Takeaway

Acceptance is not the absence of grief; it is learning to carry it with grace and honor.

Scripture (ESV)

Isaiah 61:3: "To grant to those who mourn in Zion, to give them a beautiful headdress instead of ashes, the oil of gladness instead of mourning, the garment of praise instead of a faint spirit, that they may be called oaks of righteousness, the planting of the Lord, that he may be glorified."

Prayer

Lord, thank You for the gift of my mother's life and the ways her love still shapes me. Help me live in a way that honors her and glorifies You. When the ache of missing her feels overwhelming, remind me that her story did not end; it continues in me. Amen.

Acceptance: When Joy Finally Returned

Introduction

This letter was written from a place of quiet surrender, when the waves of grief began to settle and I realized that joy and sorrow could coexist. Acceptance did not come all at once; it came softly, through unexpected moments of love and memory that reminded me God was still weaving beauty from my pain.

Letter to God

Dear God,

I never thought I could experience joy again when I thought about my mother. For so long, I was consumed by guilt, anger, and despair. I accepted those emotions as my permanent companions.

One day, while riding in the car with my daughter, something shifted. We were singing one of her favorite songs, and as I looked over at her, smiling, carefree, and bopping her head to the music, I saw myself in her. That moment took me back to my childhood, to the many times my mom and I sang our hearts out with the windows down. Suddenly, I was overwhelmed, not with sadness but with joy and gratitude.

I tried to hold back my tears so I would not ruin our karaoke session, but they came anyway. When my daughter asked, "Mommy, what is wrong?" I was finally able to say, "These are happy tears." I told her about my mom and how we used to have car karaoke sessions just like this. She smiled, held my hand, turned the music back up, and we kept singing.

As we sang, I thanked You. Thank You for giving me a daughter who carries my mother's light in her laughter. Thank You for loving me so intentionally, for the way You gave me this blessing even when I was drowning in grief. I still remember that it was the weekend of my first Mother's Day without my mom when I found out I was pregnant. I had no idea then that parenting my daughter would give me new insight into how deeply my own mother loved me.

Now, as a mother myself, I cannot imagine the pain she endured losing a child. When I think of her now, I smile. I see her strength. I see my own resilience. I went from feeling cheated by You, angry that she died just ten months after my brother, to being grateful for every day she survived such heartbreak. I am grateful that her pain is over, that she is whole again in Your presence.

Thank You for the revelation, Lord. Thank You for helping me see that grief does not erase joy, it deepens it. Acceptance does not mean forgetting; it means finally trusting that You make all things new.

Love,

Ericka

Takeaway

Acceptance is not the absence of grief; it is the quiet peace that comes when love begins to outweigh the pain. God can turn even our deepest sorrow into a gentle reminder of His faithfulness.

Scripture (ESV)

Isaiah 61:3: "To give them a crown of beauty for ashes, the oil of joy for mourning, the garment of praise for the spirit of heaviness, that they might be called trees of righteousness, the planting of the Lord, that he may be glorified."

Prayer

Lord, thank You for meeting me in my grief and teaching me that joy can return, not as a replacement for sorrow but as its companion. Thank You for showing me glimpses of Your redemption through my daughter's laughter and my mother's memory. Help me keep living from a place of gratitude, trusting that even in loss, You are still good. Amen.

Acceptance: When Silence Became Sacred

Introduction

This letter came from a place of deep stillness, a season when the noise of grief had finally quieted and I realized that silence was no longer my enemy. For so long, I filled every quiet space with activity, conversation, or distraction because I was afraid of what I might feel if I stopped. Over time, God showed me that silence can be sacred, the place where His voice becomes clear and my heart can finally rest.

Letter to God

Dear God,

There was a time when silence felt like abandonment. When the phone stopped ringing and everyone went back to their lives, I was left with the ache of what I had lost. The quiet felt heavy, like an echo of everything I wished I could change.

So I drowned myself in busyness, consuming my calendar with work and school. I was desperate to stay occupied, to avoid the silence at any cost. I remember coming home so exhausted that all I could do was shower and fall asleep, and that is exactly what I wanted. If I stayed busy, I did not have to face the pain. If I stayed tired, I did not have to feel the ache.

But something changed. Somewhere between the tears and the healing, You taught me how to breathe again in the quiet. The stillness that once felt suffocating has become holy ground. It is where I sense Your nearness most.

In the silence, I learned how to pour out my broken heart, and it was there that I felt You holding me, catching every tear. I felt the tenderness of Your love and the comfort of Your presence. I stopped trying to fill the silence because I realized You were already filling it for me.

Now, when I sit in stillness, I feel peace. I hear the soft whisper of Your presence, reminding me that I am not alone. I no longer feel pressure to perform my healing or rush my restoration. I can simply be.

In the silence, I remember my mother, not with pain but with peace. The quiet that once reminded me of her absence now reminds me of Your presence. It is where grief and grace meet.

Thank You, God, for teaching me that silence is not empty, it is a sacred space. Thank You for sitting with me in it, for holding what words could never express. You have turned what I once avoided into something holy, and in that stillness, I have found rest.

Love,

Ericka

Takeaway

Silence in grief can feel unbearable, but over time, it becomes the place where we learn to hear God again. The same stillness that once echoed with sorrow can become sacred ground for peace, reflection, and quiet communion with Him.

Scripture (ESV)

Psalm 46:10: "Be still, and know that I am God. I will be exalted among the nations, I will be exalted in the earth."

Prayer

Lord, thank You for meeting me in the quiet places. Teach me to find comfort in stillness and to recognize Your presence in the silence. Help me rest in the peace You offer, knowing that even when words fade, Your love remains. Let my heart find sacred space in the quiet with You. Amen.

Transformed by Grief

I never imagined grief would transform my relationship with God the way it has. The anger and resentment I once carried toward Him have been reshaped into deep admiration. Along this journey, I have experienced God's grace in indescribable ways.

Along the way, I realized I was grieving far more than the loss of my mom and my brother. I was grieving the version of God I thought I knew. I was grieving the life plans that would never come to pass. I was grieving the version of myself that died the day I watched their caskets lowered into the ground. I was grieving my timeline, the one that no longer existed after grief shattered it into pieces. For a long time, survival was my only focus, just putting one foot in front of the other.

Now, in my thirties, after walking through the valleys of grief and healing, I am beginning to dream and believe again. Yet even with new hope, grief still lingers. There are days when I sit with the reality that I am not where I thought I would be, that life's struggles have rerouted my plans. But what I know now is this: God's plans are always better than mine.

Through loss, I found my purpose and calling as a licensed clinical social worker and therapist. Today I have the privilege of sitting with clients as they navigate grief. I can extend a different kind of empathy, one rooted in shared understanding. They can hear in my voice and see in my eyes that I am speaking not only from training but from experience.

During my darkest nights, I prayed that God would turn my pain into purpose. He has answered that prayer in ways far beyond what I imagined. This book is one result of that transformation. My profession is another. Every day, I wake up in awe of the restoration that once felt impossible.

POUR IT OUT

If you are grieving, I want to leave you with some practical tools that helped me along the way. My prayer is that at least one of them will meet you where you are and carry you a little farther on your journey toward healing.

Practical Tips for Navigating Grief

- **Therapy** – Speaking with a trained professional gave me space to process my emotions, understand my grief, and gain tools to cope in healthy ways. My therapist and I have done great work together. Working with my therapist helped me show up more fully as a woman, wife, and mother. Therapy is not a sign of weakness; it is a courageous act of healing.
- **Prayer** – Prayer became my anchor. Some days, my prayers were long and full of words. Other days, they were nothing more than tears or a whispered, "Help me, God." All of it counted, and all of it drew me closer to Him.
- **A Support System** – Grief is heavy, and it was never meant to be carried alone. Leaning on friends, family, and my church family reminded me that I didn't have to walk through loss in isolation.
- **Honesty About Emotions** – Healing began when I gave myself permission to feel—anger, sadness, guilt, and even moments of joy. Grief is not linear. Being honest about what I was experiencing freed me from shame and allowed me to move forward.
- **Rest** – Grief is exhausting, both physically and emotionally. Rest is not laziness; it was an essential part of recovery. Giving myself grace to pause and breathe was just as important as any active step I took.
- **Purposeful Remembrance** – Finding ways to honor my mom and brother helped me keep their memory alive in a healthy way. Whether through writing, sharing stories, or small rituals, remembrance brought both comfort and meaning.

Grief will change you, but it does not have to destroy you. My prayer is that through my story, you've seen how God's grace is sufficient even in the darkest moments. May you find hope, may you feel less alone, and may you sense God's presence walking with you every step of the way.

Letters of Legacy

Dear Mama,

Where do I even begin? I miss you more than words can describe. I miss your slick mouth, your laugh, your cheesy grits, and your love. I miss your words of affirmation. You always made me feel like I could conquer the world.

Doing life without you hasn't been easy. You've missed so much, and there are countless memories I wish you could've been a part of. I wish you could've met my children—they would have adored you.

Mama, I hope and pray that I'm making you proud. I promise your hard work will never be in vain. I promise to live life to the fullest for both of us—to find the rest and peace you spent your life searching for. I promise to get that doctorate degree you always wanted for me.

Thank you for every sacrifice you made to give us a good life. Thank you for showing me what real love looks like and giving me the blueprint for how to love my own children. Thank you for being my biggest cheerleader and number-one supporter.

I'm sorry for the times I didn't show up the way I should have after Alex died. I'm sorry for the calls I missed and for the moments I didn't let you express your pain freely. It was so hard to see you hurting. The thought of losing you made me physically sick, and I just couldn't handle it while grieving Alex and trying to finish grad school. I saw you slipping away, and my heart couldn't take it.

I wish I could have been more present, more supportive. I pray you knew how deeply I loved you, even when I didn't have the strength to show it. I pray that before you left this world, you knew how much you meant to me—how valuable you were as a mother, and how much of a hero you'll always be in my eyes.

ERICKA FINLEY

I love you, Mama. Your legacy will forever live through me. You've got the best view of my life now, and there's still so much more to come. Stay tuned, Mama—I'll keep living to make you proud!

Love always,

Your daughter,

Ericka

POUR IT OUT

Dear Big Bro,

I never imagined life would turn out this way. I never thought the day would come when I couldn't just pick up the phone and call you. I'd give anything to hear you say, "What's up, Squirrel?" one more time. I'd do anything for another chance to laugh and crack jokes with you.

I miss you so much. There's so much that has happened in my life that I wish you could be a part of. Your boys are amazing—they're both just as brilliant as you were. You'd be so proud of them.

We never got the chance to have real, grown-up conversations, but as I move through life as an adult, I've gained a deeper love and respect for you—not just as my brother, but as a man. Seeing the struggles that Black men face every day has given me a new perspective when I think of you. Despite everything you were battling mentally and emotionally, you never let life steal your humor or your laughter. No matter what was going on, every time I saw you, we laughed. That joy was your superpower.

I admire the kind of father you were—present, intentional, and loving. You protected me fiercely and always believed in me. I still remember you telling your friends, "Don't talk to my sister—she's going places." You always saw the greatness in me, and you made sure no one could distract me from my purpose.

Thank you for always having my back. Thank you for loving me without conditions. Thank you for teaching me to look for joy, even in hard times, and to never let life steal my laughter. I haven't mastered that yet—but when I catch myself forgetting how to laugh, thinking of you always brings it back.

I promise to always do my best to take care of your boys. I'll always stand in proxy for you when it comes to them. Kiss Mama for me and tell her I love her.

I love you forever.

Your little sister,

Squirrel

Dear Little Sister,

Through this journey of grief, you've been the one person who truly understands the depth of my pain. I thank God often for giving me you to walk this difficult road together.

As you read these pages, I hope you've seen how the love of God has been woven through my story. My prayer is that it reminds you there is nothing too big, too broken, or too hidden for him to heal. He is ready and waiting to meet you in every place of sorrow—all you have to do is pour it out before Him.

If there is one thing I pray you carry with you, let it be hope. We may have lost our mother and our brother, but God, in His mercy, allowed us to have each other. He knew we would need one another to survive this.

There's so much you've carried quietly over the years. I see the pain in your eyes sometimes when I look at you. I believe with all my heart that God wants to meet you there—in those hidden places—to restore you and give you the healing you deserve. You often speak about how much God loves me, how blessed I am. But I want you to know this: God loves YOU just the same. His love for you is just as intentional, just as personal. It was no coincidence that God allowed you to have intimate access to my healing journey. He wanted you to see with your own eyes that healing is real—and possible.

It is my deepest prayer that you will find the courage to lay your pain at your heavenly father's feet. Every buried emotion, every silent tear, every ache you've held inside—He can carry it all. And He's waiting for you.

I love who you are today, but I also can't wait to meet the fully healed version of you. I believe she is powerful, free, and overflowing with peace.

I love you, and I'm praying for you always.

With all my heart,

Ericka

POUR IT OUT

Dear Nephews,

I love you both more than words can say. From the moment you entered this world, you've carried pieces of our family's story within you. I know life has handed you pain no child should have to carry—the loss of your dad and your grandmother. But I need you to know this: you are not defined by what you've lost. You are defined by the love, the strength, and the legacy that still flows through you.

Your father loved you deeply, and so did your grandmother. Their blood runs in your veins, their courage beats in your hearts, and their legacy will live on through the men you are becoming.

I pray you'll always remember that even in the hardest moments, God's hand is on your life. He has preserved you for a purpose greater than you can imagine. The broken pieces of your story will not stop you—they will shape you. They will remind you of where you've come from, but they will not limit where you're going.

As your auntie, I promise to keep showing up for you. I will remind you of who you are when the world tries to make you forget: you are strong, you are loved, and you are destined for greatness.

Your story is still being written, and I believe it will be filled with victory, joy, and purpose. Carry your father's laugh, your grandmother's strength, and your own unique gifts into the future. That's how their love lives on—through you.

With all my love,

Auntie Ericka

Dear Hubby,

Thank you. Those two words feel too small for everything you've been to me, but they're the only place I can begin.

You've walked beside me through the darkest valleys of my life, never rushing me, never silencing me, never letting me carry the weight alone. You have held me when I wept, prayed for me when I felt too weak to pray for myself, and reminded me of joy when I thought I had lost it forever.

Your love has been a steady anchor in the storm. In every breakdown, every sleepless night, every wave of grief, you showed me what it means to be chosen, cherished, and safe. You have been a living example of God's love—patient, kind, and unwavering.

Because of you, I never felt completely alone. Because of you, I learned it was possible to laugh again, to dream again, to hope again. Our marriage has been a testimony to me of God's faithfulness—proof that beauty can rise from ashes and that love can survive the hardest seasons.

I want you to know that I see you. I see the sacrifices you've made, the patience you've shown, the strength you've given so freely. And I don't take any of it for granted. I am forever grateful that God chose you for me.

I love you, not only for the man you are but also for the way you have loved me through my brokenness. You've been my partner, my protector, my encourager, and my safe place. Thank you for helping me see that grief doesn't have to mean the end of joy—that love can exist even in the valley.

With all my love,

Ericka

POUR IT OUT

Dear Reader,

Thank you for walking with me through these pages. My story is not just about loss—it is about love, faith, and the God who carried me when I didn't think I could take another step.

If you're holding this book, it's because grief has touched your life too. Maybe you've lost someone you love. Maybe you're still searching for answers. Maybe you feel numb, angry, or hopeless. Wherever you are in your journey, I want you to know this: you are not alone.

Grief is not a straight line. It comes in waves, sometimes soft, sometimes crushing. But even in the darkest moments, God's presence can meet you there. His love is not afraid of your tears, your questions, or even your anger. He is big enough to handle all of it.

My prayer is that as you close this book, you open your heart to the possibility of healing. Healing does not erase the love or the memory—it carries it forward in a new way. You can honor the ones you've lost by choosing to live, by choosing to hope, by choosing to love again.

Your story is not over. Your grief is not the end. There is still joy to be found, peace to be felt, and love to be given. And you don't have to walk that road alone—God will walk it with you.

I believe in your healing. I believe in your future. I pray that these pages remind you: there is life after loss, and there is a love strong enough to carry you through.

With love and hope,

Ericka

Faith & Emotional Healing Tools

This section offers gentle, faith-centered practices to help you regulate your emotions, find stillness, and remain connected to God's comforting presence as you navigate grief.

1. Breath Prayer

When emotions feel heavy, let your breath become a quiet prayer:

Inhale: *You are near.*

Exhale: *I am safe with You.*

Other options:
- Inhale: *Your peace fills me.*
- Exhale: *Your love sustains me.*

2. Scripture Meditation

Find a quiet space. Read slowly and allow one word or phrase to rest on your heart.

Suggested Passage: Psalm 23 (ESV)

"*The Lord is my shepherd; I shall not want.*

He makes me lie down in green pastures.

He leads me beside still waters.

He restores my soul.

He leads me in paths of righteousness for his name's sake.

Even though I walk through the valley of the shadow of death,

I will fear no evil, for you are with me;

your rod and your staff, they comfort me."

You may also reflect on Matthew 11:28–30 (ESV):

"Come to me, all who labor and are heavy laden, and I will give you rest. Take my yoke upon you, and learn from me, for I am gentle and lowly in heart, and you will find rest for your souls.

For my yoke is easy, and my burden is light."

3. Gratitude & Grounding Practice

Even in grief, small glimpses of grace can keep you anchored.

Write down three things that reminded you of God's faithfulness today—no matter how small.

It might be:

- A comforting memory
- A song that soothed you
- The strength to simply get out of bed

Let these moments remind you: healing doesn't mean forgetting. It means *learning to see God's hand even in the ache.*

Scriptures for Grief & Comfort (ESV)

When I Feel…	Scripture
Alone	*Deuteronomy 31:8 — "It is the Lord who goes before you. He will be with you; He will not leave you or forsake you. Do not fear or be dismayed."*
Angry or Confused	*Psalm 13:1-2 — "How long, O Lord? Will you forget me forever? How long will you hide your face from me? How long must I take counsel in my soul and have sorrow in my heart all the day? How long shall my enemy be exalted over me?"*
Weary or Empty	*Isaiah 40:31 — "But they who wait for the Lord shall renew their strength; they shall mount up with wings like eagles; they shall run and not be weary; they shall walk and not faint."*
Missing Them Deeply	*1 Thessalonians 4:13-14 — "But we do not want you to be uninformed, brothers, about those who are asleep, that you may not grieve as others do who have no hope. For since we believe that Jesus died and rose again, even so, through Jesus, God will bring with him those who have fallen asleep."*

When I Feel…	Scripture
Needing Hope	*Romans 8:18 — "For I consider that the sufferings of this present time are not worth comparing with the glory that is to be revealed to us."* *Revelation 21:4 — "He will wipe away every tear from their eyes, and death shall be no more, neither shall there be mourning, nor crying, nor pain anymore, for the former things have passed away."*
Overwhelmed by Emotion	*Psalm 61:2 — "From the end of the earth I call to you when my heart is faint. Lead me to the rock that is higher than I."*
Struggling to Trust Again	*Proverbs 3:5-6 — "Trust in the Lord with all your heart, and do not lean on your own understanding. In all your ways acknowledge him and he will make straight your paths."*
Searching for Peace	*Philippians 4:7 — "And the peace of God, which surpasses all understanding, will guard your hearts and your minds in Christ Jesus."*

Pour It Out: Personal Grief Journal

Now that you've walked with me through my journey of healing, it's your turn. Welcome to this sacred space. These pages are for you to sit with your grief, talk with God, and find comfort in His presence. There is no "right" way to grieve, only honest moments before a loving God who meets you exactly where you are. May this space become your resting place with him- a place to release what hurts, remember what matters, and slowly rediscover hope.

POUR IT OUT

How has God met you in your grief up until now?

*The Lord is near to the brokenhearted
And saves the crushed in spirit.*

Psalm 34:18 ESV

POUR IT OUT

What does grief feel like for you today?

My tears are not wasted;
They water my healing.

POUR IT OUT

What are some of your most cherished memories of your loved one that still bring light and joy even in the midst of pain?

The same God who gave me love now gives me comfort. My memories are holy ground—proof that love endures beyond this moment of pain.

POUR IT OUT

When you can't find the words, what do your tears say?

Even when I can't speak it, the Lord interprets my tears as worship, surrender, and truth.

POUR IT OUT

What have you learned about love through loss?

Love does not end; it simply changes form and finds me in new ways.

POUR IT OUT

Where do you notice God's comfort showing up in your life, even in small ways?

God's mercy meets me in the details; I am never truly alone.

POUR IT OUT

Who do you need to forgive to move forward in peace? Yourself? God? Others?

Forgiveness opens my heart for God's healing to enter freely.

POUR IT OUT

How can you honor your loved one's legacy with your words, choices, and actions?

Their love lives through me, shaping the way I give and the way I live.

POUR IT OUT

There is healing and honesty. These next few pages are meant to be a safe place for your heart to speak freely. Let your words flow—unfiltered, unedited, and full of truth.

ERICKA FINLEY

POUR IT OUT

'He will wipe every tear from their eyes. There will be no more death' or mourning or crying or pain, for the old order of things has passed away."

Revelation 21:4 NIV

Use these pages to express your heart to those you miss. You may want to write one letter or several; each is a sacred act of remembrance.

POUR IT OUT

ERICKA FINLEY

My grief has changed me, but your grace sustains me.

POUR IT OUT

This is your space to talk to God openly—your gratitude, confusion, anger, hope, and surrender. God is not offended by your honesty; He welcomes it. Begin your letter with "Dear God," and let the conversation unfold.

POUR IT OUT

ERICKA FINLEY

Surrender and Renewal

Father,

Thank you for walking with me through these pages.

For being patient with my questions, tender with my pain, and faithful even when I struggle to believe you were near.

You have seen the parts of my heart I couldn't express in words—

The exhaustion, the longing, the love that still lingers.

And yet you never turned away.

Today, I release my grief into your hands once more.

Teach me to rest in your promises and to trust that healing will come in its time.

Let this space of mourning become a garden where hope takes root again.

Help me remember that love never ends; It simply changes form.

The bond between us remains, redeemed in eternity by your grace period

As I close this journal, I don't close my heart to what you're doing.

You are making beauty from the ashes,

And I am still becoming whole in your presence.

In Jesus' name,

Amen

References

Brueggemann, Walter. *Praying the Psalms: Engaging Scripture and the Life of the Spirit.* 2nd ed. Eugene, OR: Cascade Books, 2007.

Mental Health Center Kids. (n.d.). *5 stages of grief* [Infographic]. Retrieved from https://www.mentalhealthcenterkids.com/

Card, Michael. *A Sacred Sorrow: Reaching Out to God in the Lost Language of Lament.* Colorado Springs, CO: NavPress, 2005.

Westermann, Claus. *Praise and Lament in the Psalms.* Translated by Keith R. Crim. Atlanta: John Knox Press, 1981.

The Holy Bible, English Standard Version. Wheaton, IL: Crossway Bibles, 2016.

Made in the USA
Coppell, TX
07 January 2026